# The Crisis of Christianity

## The Turning Point

Tom Molnar

I0836119

Apple Valley Press

## Also by Tom Molnar

Wired for Love: How to Make it the Best (2022)

Mist on the Moon—Fiction (2022)

Time Out for Happiness (2021)

Jesus: Kind, Loving, Dangerous (2020)

Swept Away: Of Life and Love During the American Civil War—Fiction (2020)

The Universe of God and Humanity (2019)

The Resurrection: How Everything Changed (2015)

Tara's World: A Land of Beauty, Danger, and Love—Fiction (2014)

Christianity, the Challenge of a Changing World (2012)

Dark Age Maiden—Fiction (2012)
Sequel
Dark Age Woman—Fiction (2016)

A Quick Look at Heaven (2011)

Love Stories from the Heart—Fiction (2006)

Love Strokes—Fiction (2005)

The Crisis of Christianity



ISBN 978-1-7343593-5-0



Manufactured in the United States of America

To my gracious editor whom I rely on to help point out any grammar or other mistakes. To my lovely and fortunate to have found wife with whom I have shared so much who still feels I spend too much time on the computer.

# The Crisis of Christianity

## The Turning Point

Why have people walked away from church? Why do many children of faith-filled parents not attend services? Why do many parents today feel the need to protect their children from the negative influences of society?

Though we live in a time of change, surveys show that most people still believe in God. Even those who seldom or never attend religious services often maintain some prayer life and devotion. Nevertheless, it is undeniable that in some parts of the world churches are closing and the number of Christians attending services is declining.

Why? This book will describe what has been happening in our culture and in our lives that has turned many away from their religious heritage. And yet, going forward, there is reason for hope.

## Contents

1. God through the Ages 9

2. Today's Two Largest Religions 13

3. Founders of the Great Monotheistic Religions 17

4. The Phenomenal Growth of Christianity 24

5. The Growth of Islam 31

6. The Age of Faith: Good Times and Bad 34

7. Manorial Life 42

8. The Changes Begin: Early Modern Europe and America 51

9. Some Thoughts on Evolution 56

10. Seeing God in the Scientific Era of Today 59

11. A Beautiful but not Perfect World 67

12. Suffering 71

13. Religion Today 75

14. Social Media: Positives and Negatives 82

15. Protecting Children: Then and in Today's World 87

16. A New Beginning 97

17. On Living the Good Life 103

18. God's Relationship with Us 109

19. Why People Do and Don't Go to Church 112

20. Epilogue 118

Note 126

Today, young and old are often immersed in pervasive media. All of us receive national, local and personal information through our phones, our TVs and through media outlets such as Facebook, (Meta), Twitter, Instagram, TikTok, Snapchat, and a host of others. Except for TV, all this has come about since the turn of the century. Not surprisingly, none of the top ten social media sites is spiritually orientated. Today, more people have become atheists and some popular authors write books maintaining that there is no God.

Why has this happened and what will be the future? Long ago, Jesus warned his contemporaries to be on the alert for “false prophets.” His words apply just as well today. Yes, God is not dead, but we may need a reintroduction. He is far more alive and active than we may realize.

# God through the Ages

Despite a modern tendency among some to debunk God, He has been part of our heritage since the beginning of human history. There is substantial evidence that even in prehistoric times, before humans learned to write, the dead were buried in ways showing respect for the body and belief in an afterlife. In historical times, every known human culture, the first arising in Mesopotamia, has had its god or gods as well as rituals to honor their god and to ask for favorable outcomes for crops and for personal needs.

Personally, I was raised as a Catholic Christian and therefore taught to believe in God. However, early on I loved science fiction as well as science in general so tended to look at God and the world from a scientific point of view. This did not help me in a religion class when a good Christian brother was explaining aspects of faith. My hand shot up repeatedly, probably much to the chagrin of the teacher as well as my classmates. The problem was that I was trying arduously to understand things rationally that are more easily accepted through faith. I guess that's how I am, always trying to think things through. Definitely not one who shines at small talk but in a deeper conversation I'm all in. Yes, that's how I have proceeded, from when I was an army electronic technician to today, making sense of the world and our place in it. In my far-ranging studies, I've learned much about the world of science, about the Bible, God and Jesus Christ and about life in a changing world. Not that I or anyone else knows all the answers to life in our complex universe.

The first and possibly the most interesting historical civilization developed in Mesopotamia. There, the ancient Sumerian civilization, arising in present day Iraq began. Nearby is where the Garden of Eden is thought to have existed, based on the description provided in Genesis 2:8-14. Sumerian culture goes back in its earliest times to almost 6000 BC. Their towns were well positioned near and between the Tigris and Euphrates Rivers which was the source of their water supply, their fishing activities, and most of all, the rivers that supplied water for farming their crops in the otherwise semiarid region. The alluvial soils deposited in the springtime when the rivers were high provided annual nourishment for their fruits and vegetables.

For enjoyment, they were the first culture to learn to make beer and they also made various kinds of stringed musical instruments. In addition, they were the first to make a sailboat and to fashion objects of copper including containers for water and food, statues and arrowheads. A major achievement of theirs was to develop a manually turned wheel which allowed them to mass produce pottery used for all manner of dinnerware and for large containers to hold foods such as beans, chick peas, cucumbers and wheat.

What is most interesting is that the Sumerians, similarly to the Bible, also write about an ancient flood and a chosen man who was instructed to build a large boat to save those on board from the ravages of the waters. The similarities of the Sumerian flood to Noah and the flood in Genesis is surprising and may well have been inspired by the same event. As told in their written story, the Epic of Gilgamesh, the flood was brought on by man's wickedness. Both Noah and Utnapishtim were ordered to build a huge boat. Each of the boats was several stories high and carried, besides family members, all variety of animals and seeds for planting. According to the Epic of Gilgamesh, the Sumerian flood lasted only six days while in the Bible the flood of Noah lasted for forty. However, in both stories birds were released in an attempt to find dry land. And finally, both vessels landed on a mountain, though the two mountains are almost 300 miles apart.

As for their worship, the Sumerians, like all of the ancient civilizations of which we have knowledge, worshiped many gods. In fact, it has been found that thousands of gods appear in their cuneiform writing. There were the gods of each of their major cities as well as many that are linked to specific families. The pattern of having many gods continued with the Egyptians and then with the Greek and Roman pantheon of gods. However, long before the cultures that became Greece and Rome, the Bible tells that Abram was told by God to leave the great metropolis of the Sumerian city of Ur sometime about 2066 BC. According to the Bible, God told Abram (later Abraham) to leave Ur to found a new nation that was to worship only one God. That nation subsequently became Israel. Abraham became the first of the Hebrew patriarchs, a figure today revered by the three great monotheistic religions—Judaism, Christianity and Islam.

## Today's Two Largest Religions

Today, religions that believe in only one God comprise well over half of the world's population. Christianity is the largest of these by number, according to Pew research, with approximately 2.4 billion adherents. Christianity is itself divided by numbers into Catholic, then Protestant and then Eastern Orthodox Christianity. Islam is next in size with approximately 1.9 billion adherents and Judaism comprises only about 15 million members. Christianity is spread throughout the world and has great numbers of adherents in Africa and North and South America. Islam is a religion of much of the Middle East, upper Africa, and South and Southeast Asia. However, Islam is growing faster than Christianity mainly because Muslims have larger families on average than Christians. Because of birth rates, it is anticipated that sometime later in this century Islam may become the most populous religion on earth.

What are the differences in the sacred writings of these religions? The main work of Christianity is the Bible, both the Old and the New Testament. Judaism counts as authentic only the Old Testament and does not accept the New Testament. The Jewish religion doesn't believe that Christ is God. The religion of Islam has, at least for Christians and Jews, an unusual interpretation of Biblical scripture.

According to conventional Islamic belief, the Quran, their main holy book, was revealed to the Prophet Muhammad by the angel Gabriel. The pages of the Quran include many of the same people that are found in the Hebrew Bible including stories of Adam, Noah, Abraham, Lot, Isaac, Ishmael, Jacob, Joseph, Moses, David and Goliath, and Jonah. Mary, the mother of Jesus, and John the Baptist all appear in the Quran, as does Jesus.

These major personages and something of their lives are part of the many shared narratives found in both the Quran and the Bible. Among the stories of the Bible that are also included in the Quran are the Garden of Eden, the flood, God's choice of Abraham to found the nation of Israel and Abraham's near-sacrifice of one of his sons. Also included in the holy book of Islam are the story of Moses and the exodus of the Israelites from Egypt, the life and death of Jesus, and the idea that God repeatedly sends prophets to warn and instruct mankind.

The Quran also includes stories from some early apocryphal gospels, like that of the Gospel of Thomas, showing Jesus as a child bringing clay birds to life by breathing on them and even that Jesus could speak as a prophet from the cradle (from the Syriac Apocryphal Infancy Gospel). However, the teachings of Jesus, his parables and healings do not appear in the Quran. Also missing are the narratives of the life of Jesus, his teachings and miracles, which make up so much of the New Testament but are absent in the Quran. In fact, one very important difference is that in the Quran Jesus is not crucified but is saved from the cross by a special act of God.

Another major change seen in the Quran is the total elimination of any women by name from their scripture with the exception of Mary, the mother of God. Even Eve is not mentioned by name. There is no Ruth, Rachel, Deborah, Rebekah, Judith, Esther, or even Jezebel as well as many other women. In the Quran, Mary's mother, Anne doesn't appear and there is also no mention of Martha and Mary, Salome, Mary Magdalene, and the woman at the well, etc. The Quran is a smaller book than the Bible, consisting of about 600 pages, compared to the Bible's over 1200 pages. Nevertheless, the Quran's almost total elimination of women is surprising.

# Founders of the Great Monotheistic Religions

There are some similarities between Christianity and Islam. One of the main similarities is that both religions worship one God. What about the founders of these religions? Let's start with Mohammad.

## Mohammad

Mohammad, also spelled Muhammad, was born in 570 AD in Mecca in western Saudi Arabia. His father died before he was born and he was raised by Amina, his mother, until she also died when he was six years old. The young Mohammad was then placed in the care of his paternal grandfather, Abd al-Mutalib. Then, about two years later, Mohammad's grandfather died and he was next cared for by his uncle, Abu Talib. Early on, Mohammad worked as a shepherd, but in his teens, he traveled with his uncle, a merchant, by caravan to various and sometimes distant trade centers.

By the time he reached his twenties Mohammad found employment with a wealthy Meccan merchant named Khadija. A widow, Khadijah was impressed with the young man's abilities and character such that she proposed marriage to him though he was only twenty-five and she was forty. Mohammad had six children with Khadijah but their two sons both died in infancy.

Mohammad had learned something about Judaism and Christianity in his many travels as a merchant. He began to turn away from the many gods fostered in the city of Mecca, his hometown. It is recorded that he began making long retreats to a mountain cave just outside the city. It was then that he began to feel an overpowering presence instructing him to recite words of special importance. Over the next 23 years he continued to receive these words which have been attributed to the Angel Gabriel. They were subsequently written down by scribes under the direction of Abu Bakr, Mohammad's friend and advisor. The sum of the revelations became the Muslim holy book, the Quran.

The next part of Mohammad's life is difficult to briefly summarize. He began gathering followers who also believed in one God but found himself opposed by the leaders of Mecca who not only believed in many gods but also were profiting from visitors coming to the places of worship of these gods. A number of battles ensued both with Mecca and with Jewish and other communities. Mohammad himself led many expeditions and surprisingly, besides his prophetic role, he was also a good military leader. His wife Khadijah died in 619 and he subsequently took nine wives. It is said that he gave them protection during those uncertain times. Mohammad himself died in 632 of natural causes after a brief illness.

What is clear is that militarily the Muslims soon became the most powerful force in the known world. In less than 100 years after Mohammad's death they conquered most of the Middle East, failing only in their attack on Constantinople, the "New Rome" in 718. By that time, they had conquered all the states of North Africa, defeated Spain and occupied part of southern Europe until they were turned back in present day France in the famous Battle of Tours in 732. Even today, much of the area of their conquests remains Muslim.

# Jesus

Biblical scholars believe that Jesus was born in Israel between 6 BC and 4 BC. According to the New Testament he was born of the virgin Mary in the small town of Bethlehem. Mary and Joseph had traveled a distance of about 90 miles from Nazareth to pay the Roman taxes, which required them to return to the town of Joseph's heritage. The family stayed in Bethlehem for a time after Christ's birth, but later left for Egypt to escape King Herod's massacre of the innocents as described by the Gospel of Matthew 2:13-23. After Herod's death the family returned to Nazareth where Jesus learned the trade of carpentry from Joseph and worked at the occupation until he was approximately thirty years of age. The Gospels don't indicate when Joseph died, but Christ's ministry is thought to have begun sometime after his death. It was then that he began his teaching and worked the many miracles that are recorded in the Gospels. Most of Christ's miracles were the healing of those with various kinds of sickness, including lepers, a man born blind, a paralytic, a man with a withered hand, and many more. He also raised three people from the dead. His first recorded miracle was turning water into wine at a wedding feast, an important event at least to the bride and groom, for Jewish wedding feasts ordinarily lasted for days.

At the time that Jesus was living in Israel, the ritual laws of the Jews had become quite complex such that they were hard for most Jews to follow. The Pharisees, the religious leaders, insisted that all the laws should all be followed. Christ's violation of some of them, including their proscription against even the work of healing on the Sabbath got him into trouble with the scribes and Pharisees. Although Jesus never rescinded the law of Moses and the ten commandments, Jesus wanted to simplify man's relationship to God beyond following the profusion of rules that had entered into Jewish religion. When asked what is the greatest commandment, he summed them up saying "Love the Lord your God with all your heart and with all your soul and with all your mind. This is the first and greatest commandment. And the second is like it: Love your neighbor as yourself." (Mark 12:30,31)

It appears that Jesus wanted his followers to enter into a direct relationship with God himself. The only prayer that he is known to have taught his followers, termed the "Lord's Prayer" or the "Our Father" is specifically addressed to God who is almost affectionately titled "father." It's a simple prayer and these are its words:

"Our father, who art in heaven, hallowed be thy Name, thy kingdom come, thy will be done, on earth as it is in heaven. Give us this day our daily bread and forgive us our trespasses, as we forgive those who trespass against us. And lead us not into temptation, but deliver us from evil."

Jesus' emphasis on forgiveness in this prayer was an important aspect of his teaching. When Peter asked him, "Lord how many times should I forgive my brother when he sins against me? Up to seven times?" Jesus answered him, "I tell you not seven times but seventy-seven times." (Some Bible versions of Matthew 18:22 say "seventy times seven.")

Jesus was well received by the general population who listened to him and they sometimes even traveled long distances to hear him speak. However, the Jewish religious leaders, particularly the scribes and Pharisees, began to unite against him because he was not following the multitude of Jewish religious laws that they expected a prophet to follow. As examples of this, Jesus conversed with women not of his family (socially not acceptable at that time), touched lepers, healed on the Sabbath, ate with sinners and tax collectors and stopped the stoning of a woman caught in adultery. However, what incensed them the most was when Jesus made this statement: "I and the Father are one." (John 10:30) At that, many of those listening picked up stones to kill him, but Jesus slipped away from them.

Jesus' claim to be one with God the Father ultimately led to his crucifixion. The religious authorities claimed to Pontius Pilate that Jesus had said he was "the king of the Jews." As the Romans had subjugated the country many years before, to Pilate there could be no other authority except his own and that of the Roman Emperor, Tiberius Caesar Augustus. Ultimately, Christ was crucified. His resurrection on the third day and appearance to his disciples and many others was the start of the religion known as Christianity.

At first, the religion grew somewhat slowly, but before long it was spread to many lands by the apostles, most of whom died for the faith. For over 250 years Christianity endured periodic deadly persecutions in the Roman Empire until in 313 AD the Edict of Milan permanently established religious toleration for Christianity.

# The Phenomenal Growth of Christianity

We will start with Christianity, the oldest of the two largest religions in the world. Early on, the apostles and the early church gained many supporters from those who converted from Judaism. However, Christianity was from the start a persecuted religion. Stephen, a deacon of the young church was the first martyr, stoned to death by the Jews. The apostles Peter and John were soon arrested and put in prison, only to be released when their chains fell off as is described in the Acts of the Apostles. Saul, before his conversion, was one of the Pharisees who went about arresting and putting Christians in prison. Many Christians fled Jerusalem to escape persecution. Some of them went to Damascus, and that is where Saul and his companions were going with a mandate from the high priest to arrest Christians and bring them back to Jerusalem as prisoners. As is recorded in the Acts, Saul was blinded on the journey to Damascus and heard a voice asking, "Saul, Saul, why do you persecute me?" When Saul asked who was speaking, the answer came, "I am Jesus, whom you are persecuting."

The story of Saul's conversion and his taking the name Paul is recorded in the Acts of the Apostles. (Acts 9:8) Christian people were at first afraid of him, but in the years that followed, Paul became one of the greatest leaders of the new church. He himself suffered many tribulations including stoning, imprisonment and finally martyrdom in Rome where he had gone to preach the new religion.

Rome was the largest and most important city of the world in the first century AD. Estimates are that in that century approximately one million people lived in Rome. Early on, some Jews had gone there on business, exporting among other things salted and dried fish from the sea of Galilee. Others went there to take up residence during the Jewish persecution of Christians. Still other Christians went to Rome to tell people of Christ. Among them were the apostles Peter and Paul. For a time, things went well, until Nero became the emperor. Then, in June of 64 AD, a huge fire broke out in Rome that destroyed or severely damaged 10 of the 14 districts of Rome.

Nero blamed the fire on Christians and began a severe persecution of them. Christians were arrested, tortured, executed, fed to wild dogs and crucified. Among them were St. Peter, who died head down on a cross and St. Paul who was beheaded. Nero is considered one of the worst if not the worst emperor of Rome. He murdered his mother, his first wife and likely his second as well as many others besides the great number of Christians that he executed.

Unfortunately, although Nero started the persecution of Christians, his example was followed by many other emperors of Rome. Yet, under some of the many Roman rulers in the next 250 years, Christians could live their lives free from danger. However, under other emperors they could be imprisoned, tortured and killed if they were known to be Christians or refused to offer a libation to one of the Roman gods. How could a persecuted religion survive? It is surprising that through the various persecutions the number of Christian adherents continued to grow. Obviously, there was something about the religion of Jesus Christ that in the hedonistic tending Roman Empire was attractive to the people. Instead of the Roman entertainment spectacles where gladiators fought to the death, Christians preached and lived love of neighbor. Instead of cruel public executions where men and sometimes women suffered for hours or even for a day or more on a cross, Christians remembered Jesus who also died on a cross and then rose again.

There is another important reason that over a span of two and a half centuries the Christian population continued to grow in the Roman Empire in both numbers and in percentage of the population. It was not at all uncommon for Romans to practice infanticide. Boys were generally preferred and many girl babies were either killed or left outside to die. Richard Stark, in his book *The Rise of Christianity* documents that oftentimes Christian women who found babies left out to die would take them and raise them in their own families as Christians. The general preference of many Romans for male children ultimately meant that there were fewer women to be wed which over time had the effect of reducing the birth rate among non-Christian families.

Christians in the Roman Empire suffered one final major persecution under Diocletian in 303 AD. Besides his cruelty to Christians, Diocletian is also known for dividing the Roman Empire into two parts. Rome remained the center of the Western Empire while Byzantium, soon to be renamed Constantinople, became the center of the Eastern Roman empire. Diocletian himself ruled in the east and appointed Maximian to rule the west. However, in 312 Constantine defeated Maximian's son, Maxentius, and thus became the Western Roman emperor.

The next year, in 313 AD, Constantine proclaimed that every person was "free to follow the religion which he chooses." With that edict, suddenly Christians were able to live their lives free from persecution. They built churches, monasteries and care facilities for the sick that would later become hospitals. The church began to send missionaries to the far-flung parts of the empire and beyond. Christianity suddenly saw huge growth within the empire and in 380 AD Christianity was decreed to be the state religion of the Roman Empire. However, the western empire was already in decline and less than one hundred years later Rome fell to Germanic invaders. The Christianized Roman Empire of the east, centered in Constantinople, lasted for another thousand years until it was defeated by the Ottoman Empire in 1453.

Despite the fall of Rome, Christianity continued to grow within the former empire and by 600 AD most of the people professed the Catholic faith. Significantly, after the fall, church prelates in Rome and in many other towns of the former empire took up administrative responsibilities that helped to carry on many aspects of the Roman culture. Latin was the language of the western empire and remained the language of administrative proceedings as well as the language of the Catholic Church. In fact, throughout much of the world Latin was retained in the ritual of the Mass until 1965. In the Eastern Roman Empire Greek was both the administrative language and for many people the common language.

The spread of Christianity throughout the former Roman empire and beyond was brought about through missionaries sent to various lands. St. Patrick's missionary work in Ireland beginning in 432 AD was successful and, later in the century, the conversion of King Clovis I helped to spread Christianity in the region now known as France. St. Augustine and a team of missionaries were sent by Pope Gregory the Great to present day England in 596 AD and in the next century St Boniface began his missionary work among Germanic tribes. These are only a few of the many missionaries, some, who like St. Boniface, lost their lives in their endeavors. As for forced conversions, there is not much information available on that, although Charlemagne is believed to have forced the Germanic people known as Saxons to give up their pagan gods and become Christian. There is likewise record of a number of instances when Jews living in some German territories were forcefully converted. However, it appears that in general, for the vast majority of peoples, conversion was not by force of arms but through acceptance. However, perhaps not surprisingly, some popular pagan customs continued to be practiced by many peoples for a long time along with the new Christianity.

# The Growth of Islam

As mentioned, In the short space of 100 years Islam succeeded in reaching much of the known world. Islam is today the second largest religion in the world. The beginning of Islam goes back to 610 AD at the time when Mohammad had retired to his cave and an angelic presence came over him. At first, he encountered much resistance but ultimately those close to him came to believe in his message of one God, Allah.

As the message of Mohammad spread, resistance grew but eventually he was able to win over many followers. The important city of Mecca was in particular opposed to the new religion but Mohammad led a large armed force and was able to impose his will on the leaders of the city. As other areas in the Arabian

Peninsula resisted the Islamic movement, Mohammad and his followers set about to spread the new faith throughout much of the Western Arabian Peninsula by conversion and military force. By the time of his death in 632 AD he had conquered much of the Arabian Peninsula for Allah. In 632 AD Mohammad died, leaving no heir.

For a short time, there was some uncertainty about who should lead after Mohammad, but soon Abu Bakr, his close friend as well as father-in-law, continued in the steps of Mohammad. He successfully finished compiling the Quran and set about spreading the message of Allah by force of arms as well as by peaceful methods. He lived only a short time after Mohammad but did choose a successor. Umar ibn Al-Khattab and the next three successors to Mohammad, or Caliphs, (the word caliph means successor), conquered by force of arms much of the Eastern Roman Empire including Syria, Jerusalem and Egypt as well as Iraq and Iran.

The Omayyad Caliphate which followed had by 750 AD extended the borders of Islam east beyond Iraq and Iran into India and Afghanistan and west across North Africa and into Spain. At its largest, the Muslim Empire extended throughout an area double the maximum size of the Roman Empire and greater in area than the length and breadth of the United States. A major reason for the success of the Islamic military was the relative vacuum of political and military power during their expansion. The Western Roman Empire was gone by this time and the Eastern Empire, centered in Constantinople, had fought the Sassanians, the former Persians, to a virtual stalemate with much loss of life and resources.

There is another major reason for the Muslim success. The people in the towns and countries that capitulated to Muslim rule, in particular "People of the Book," that is Christians and Jews, were for the most part allowed to continue their own religious services. They did not have to convert to the religion of Islam. However, there was one major stipulation. Non-Islamic people were required to pay a poll tax, the Jizya, with some exceptions made for the poor, and the handicapped. The expansion of Muslim power had happened so quickly that for a long time, as much as for hundreds of years in some areas, most of the people they ruled over were not of Islamic faith. However, as time went on, the Muslim faith was accepted by more and more people, many with genuine conversion, though others may have done so to avoid having to pay the poll tax on those not of the Muslim religion.

# The Age of Faith: Good Times and Bad

Throughout history humans have wanted to worship a deity. This is apparent from what we know of the earliest civilizations. Today, there are some who seem to want to dispense with God and others who profess no belief whatever. William Durant's fourth volume of the history of mankind is titled "The Age of Faith." For we who live in an age where faith is ridiculed by some and abandoned by others, what was it like to live in an era when faith was practically universal? We will take a look at that and then later we will be able to compare life then to life today in a much more secular world. So, other than the obvious material differences, how was life and thought different from today? And, more importantly, were people happy in those times?

Anyone can pick up a book on life in the Middle Ages that at minimum is somewhat descriptive of the conditions of life in those times. We won't do that here, for that would be a book in itself. However, let's quickly outline the general conditions prevalent beginning in the fifth and continuing through fifteenth centuries and then take a look at how people lived their lives under the prevailing conditions. We will assume a time of peace, for war always makes life more difficult both in times past and in modern times.

## General Conditions in Medieval Times

1) Except for Spain, conquered by the Muslims, the Roman Catholic Church was only church in Europe until 1054 AD when the Eastern Orthodox Church split from the Catholic Church.

2) Most healthcare, within the limits of the times, was provided by the church.

3) Until the later Middle Ages most people lived on a manor, which could be large or small.

4) The church set limits on warfare

5) The church also provided the majority of education, with the exception of private tutors, including the founding and staffing of universities.

6) Much entertainment was provided by the church.

7) Before Galileo and Copernicus, most people believed that heaven and the angels were to be found directly above the earth.

Some of the above statements may need support, for most of us are not students of medieval history. In regard to the first, during the medieval period there was until the fourteenth century only the Catholic and the Orthodox form of Christianity. Then in the fourteenth century John Wycliffe and Jan Hus began Christian reform movements preaching against corruption and the sale of indulgences within the church. Martin Luther, who in 1517 successfully broke from the church, established the Lutheran Church as a major form of Christianity. This was the situation of religion in

Europe until other branches of Protestantism developed. However, during the Middle Ages, after 700 AD, Islam had already become the dominant religion in Spain as well as the northern part of Africa and the Middle East.

As for education, Latin and religion were the main subjects taught in monastic and in cathedral schools. Later in the Middle Ages universities developed and added other courses such as math and rhetoric as well some training in science. Most of the universities that were formed were linked to bishoprics and the majority of the teachers were clergymen. However, with a few exceptions, it was only the well to do parents, that is, mostly nobility, who could send their children to school. And by and large it was only boys who were afforded the opportunity. Those who would become priests and clergy needed to be able to read and understand Latin, the written language of the Middle Ages.

Similarly, nobility needed to be educated in order to manage their often vast estates. For the great majority of the population there was actually little need for education. The printing press had not yet been invented and any literature available was painstaking copied by monks such that each copy was priceless or quite expensive. It was unlikely that anyone other than the clergy or nobility would have access to or could afford to buy written books of any kind. Of course, one did not need to know how to read and write to farm, to keep house or to engage in any number of craft occupations. At least 90 to 95 percent of the medieval population was illiterate and few would in any event have had access to written material.

The Church's influence on the conduct of arms came about in reaction to the internecine fighting that ensued in some parts of Europe with the rise of knighthood. It was a way of mitigating the general lawlessness that arose in areas of Europe where there was no strong government and instead a multitude of small kingdoms fighting for power. The "Peace of God" movement originated in 975 AD and prohibited fighting on Sundays and feast days. It also restricted combatants from harming churches, monasteries, clergy, merchants and from violating women and burning the houses of peasants. Some years later the "Truce of God" was initiated which further limited the number of days fighting could be conducted. The penalty for violation of these injunctions was excommunication from all the sacraments and services of the church. Later in the Middle Ages, a code of chivalry arose in association with the medieval Christian institution of knighthood with its attendant virtues of courage, honor, courtesy, justice and readiness to help the weak.

Similarly, the church took the lead in what healthcare was available. Modern medicine, which developed mainly in the 1900's, was unknown and as a result it was a tragic fact of life that babies and young children often died of childhood diseases. The Roman Empire which preceded the Middle Ages had no real hospitals although they did have some care facilities for wounded gladiators and for Roman soldiers. It was only after the Christian persecution ended in the fourth century AD that bishops established care facilities for the general population. These later sometimes developed into hospitals.

Another source that provided care was monasteries. After the fall of the Roman Empire continental Europe saw a tremendous growth in the number of monasteries. The monks who lived in the buildings they constructed dedicated themselves to prayer and to hard work. Monks would do different jobs according to their talents or aptitudes. Some would be engaged in growing food for the community or raising domestic animals, others would weave clothing and still others would laboriously hand- copy books such as the Bible as well as books of antiquity written by the Greeks and Romans. Washing clothing, cooking, making wine or beer and doing repairs were other ordinary jobs that were done by monks such that most of the monasteries were completely self-sufficient. The monks celebrated mass and vespers, sang in church choirs and took vows of poverty, chastity and obedience.

In addition, monks were very helpful to those in nearby communities. In an age when inns were mostly nonexistent, monasteries provided short term accommodations and took in sick people and helped nurse them to health. At that time in history there was some knowledge of healthful herbs and potions they could administer. Also, rest, care, and the good food supplied through the monastery gardens and livestock may have restored many to health. Many of the monasteries also ran schools for youth that taught reading, writing and knowledge of the Christian faith. In the mostly illiterate society of the Middle Ages, monks, clergy, nuns and nobles were often the only people who could read and write.

Many sources indicate that most people did without medical care and instead relied on prayers, superstitious spells and folk remedies that were passed on from generation to generation. Midwives seem at all times to have been available to help women in childbirth, a process that, for most of the Middle Ages, men were barred from witnessing. The practice of medicine gradually did improve and schools for medical training became available by the eleventh century in some of the major cities. However, surprisingly it was mostly barbers who took on the additional role of pulling bad teeth and setting bones, a relatively common necessity because of the many battles that were fought by knights and sometimes by peasantry.

# Manorial Life

How and where did most people live? Early on, after the fall of Rome and until the later Middle Ages, most people lived on a manor. This is where they lived, worked and practiced their religion. Manors had actually been an important part of Roman life and were in reality country estates owned by wealthy landowners who utilized slaves or hired people to work the land and produce crops that supplied the city of Rome and other major urban centers. During the time of the Roman Empire the people who actually worked the land were the coloni. They were tenant farmers who had to pay the wealthy landowner a portion of their crops in exchange for use of the land.

Originally, the manors produced agricultural crops for Roman cities and towns. However, as life became generally more treacherous with the invasions of foreign peoples, the lords of the manors began to fortify their holdings. The people the Romans called barbarians, including the Vandals, Alani, Suebi, Burgundians, Alemanni, Goths and others were overrunning the countryside. In response to the imminent danger, the lords fenced in and then walled in their grand houses, their stables and the workshops of the carpenter, the stone mason, the blacksmith and other important crafts.

Threatened on every side from incursions of armed bands traveling in small or large groups, independent farmers sought the protection afforded by the sovereigns of the manors. The lords had by this time incorporated fighting men of their own to deal with the general lawlessness following the decline and final collapse of the Roman Empire. Gradually, as former Roman cities were overtaken by the barbarians, those who escaped from the towns also sought the protection of the rulers of the manors.

By the end of the fifth century trade between Rome and other towns was brought almost to a standstill. No longer able to obtain what they needed by trading, the manors turned to producing more basic crops to sustain all the people living on the manor. They became self-sufficient, having within their walls carpenters, bakers, blacksmiths, cloth makers, and sometimes pottery makers as well as, usually, a church. In time, villages formed outside the walls of the manor with the peasants building for themselves one or two room houses. For hundreds of years these mainly farming villages survived. The peasants and a few freeholders supplied the labor to plant and care for the crops on the large fields of the lords and their families and also worked their own smaller plots near their houses. They plowed, planted, pulled weeds and finally harvested the crops.

The people who lived in the shadow of the manors were mostly in a subservient position. To a great extent they relinquished their autonomy for the protection afforded by the lord of the manor and his fighting men.

Conditions varied widely on different manors. Over hundreds of years some manors increased tremendously in size and became prominent sites with fortresses and even castles attesting to the wealth and power of the noble and his retinue of knights. For the peasants, life didn't change a great deal, but with size often came a measure of civic pride as well as more opportunities for social life.

With the exception of Spain, everyone in Europe was either Roman Catholic or Eastern Orthodox Christian before the Reformation. For the most part, royalty and leading ladies attended the same religious services as peasants, though they ordinarily had the best reserved seating. Nobility and peasants heard the same sermons and observed the same traditional feast days and holy days of the church. Rich and poor suffered from most of the same maladies, and given the limited medical knowledge of the time, they died from the same diseases and ailments.

The church focused on the temporary nature of life on earth and on the reality of heaven and the afterlife. However, that didn't prevent people from trying to have fun in the present life.

One thing that helped was the huge number of church feast days observed by both the rich and the poor, far more than are observed today. Most of these were also days off from work. It was expected that all would attend Mass in the morning on those days, but for the most part, the rest of the day was free. On other days peasants would work hard using plows and oxen to get the soil ready for planting each season. The planting and the harvest seasons were especially busy times in the agricultural year when women and even young children were often employed to assist in the work and in harvesting the crop.

## Recreation

Although farming in the age before machinery tended to be arduous, there were times of the year, particularly in winter, when people could take their leisure. Women, of course, at all times of the year were engaged in caring for children, preparing meals and usually also in spinning cloth as well as tending to household domestic animals. A book has been written, *The Overworked American: The Unexpected Decline of Leisure,* by Juliet Schor, which makes the case that medieval people worked considerably less hours of the day and in the year than Americans. They generally took longer at breakfast and lunch than we do, and because agriculture is seasonal, they had many days in winter and some in summer when there was not a lot to be done on the farm. However, it is well to note that Europeans even today receive far more time off for vacation days than is customary for Americans.

So, what did they do with all their free time? And, the more important question may be, did they have fun? Obviously, they didn't have computers, television, cellphones, radio or any of the modern apps that bring us news from around the world as well as help us stay connected with friends and family. However, medieval people knew their neighbors well and also were quite familiar with village craftsmen such as the local carpenter, blacksmith, mill grinder, baker, etc. These were the people they worked beside in the fields or who might have fixed their farm equipment, ground their grain to make flour or produced wonderful tasting baked goods that they might enjoy on occasion.

It wasn't lack of interest but lack of communication that kept people from knowing much about what was going on in other areas of the country. However, when a traveler did come by, he was welcomed at table and people listened eagerly to what he had to say about how things were in other places.

Medieval people had a surprising number of things they could do in their free time. Children would play tag, blind man's bluff, ring around the Rosie and marbles. They often had dolls, plus leather and wooden balls they used for games, and a variety of spinning tops. Girls could play house and at an early age be helpful both in the house and outside in the family garden. Both girls and boys were often placed in charge of a family's domestic animals and in some parts of Europe they learned to fish and even to become proficient in the use of bows and arrows.

Adults as well as children enjoyed swimming in the warmer seasons of the year and both youths and many of the men enjoyed wrestling. Another sport that became popular and was played by groups of men was kicking a stuffed leather ball. Teams would form and the object was to advance the ball forward, similar to soccer, except that the distance to the "goal" could be a mile apart or even as far as the next village. These tended to be roughhouse affairs, and were discouraged in many areas because of the risk of injury.

Of course, everyone enjoyed dining, especially when sometimes on celebrated feast days delicious food became available thanks to the generosity of the lord of the manor or the church. Peasants would have known each other well and likely enjoyed many friendships for they attended the same church, worked together on the same lord's fields, and attended each other's weddings and funerals.

Many paintings from hundreds of years ago show peasants feasting at big tables outdoors or dancing to a musician on the occasion of a wedding or other significant event. Usually, they enjoyed beer or ale with their dinner though wine was more common in Italy and southern France. It is not known how many, but some of the peasants brewed their own beverages. As for music, nobles and ladies had the resources to purchase and learn to play the main instruments of the day, the lute (similar to a guitar), the flute, horns, harps, drums and bagpipe as well as the church organ. Some of the peasants may have made their own instruments and by 1100 AD when travel was safer much of Europe enjoyed the visits of wandering minstrels who went from village to village playing their instruments, singing, telling stories or doing acrobatics similar to the street musicians and buskers of today.

In the almost total absence of media, people were hungry for stories and for news. Anyone who came from another place who would tell the of goings on in other areas was welcomed at table and could usually count on a free meal and even lodging. Especially popular were those who told engaging stories of adventure and romance. It is known that the story of Robin Hood, who stole from the rich to give to the poor, was a popular story told by minstrels long before the tale became a novel and then a movie.

The foregoing tells something of the life of medieval peasants who were far and away the vast majority of the population throughout Europe. However, in their main occupation, farming, they were not that much different from the majority of people in colonial America who were also farmers. However, they were not independent farmers like many Americans. They needed to work together to plant, to care for the crops and to bring in the harvest.

Were they happy? Certainly, they were beset with many vicissitudes, including loved ones dying at a younger age than is common today. Death tended to come much earlier in our own colonial times. One thing seems certain—they were not lonely. Everyone was expected to partake in the work that needed to be done, including children. They lived a very social life compared to today, sharing much of the same or similar work, attending the same church, celebrating feast days, weddings, and other important occasions, among them Christmas and Easter. Like most of us they enjoyed music, dancing, singing, good food and drink and conversation. Like us they worried at times about the future, of war, of crop failure, and about the health of their family and friends.

Having no phones, TV, or screens of any kind they filled much of their free time expressing themselves by speaking their thoughts with family, friends and most likely with anyone who would listen. They had time to daydream, to pray, and to think about their own death and what might happen after death. For most people, as they were all of one faith, the Church's teaching that there was an afterlife in heaven for faithful Christians must have been comforting.

# The Changes Begin: Early Modern Europe and America

We move away now from the Middle Ages to what is called the "early modern" period in Europe. Beginning in the sixteenth century major changes were occurring that would affect the lifestyle and the point of view of many. Some of these changes still affect us today. Although most of Europe was still agrarian, cities were growing in size and importance and many former peasants, or serfs, struck out to make a life for themselves in the growing towns and cities.

New discoveries were made that in sum would make educated people, mainly those who could read and write, begin to look at life in a different way. Major findings by Copernicus, Galileo and Newton in particular gave people a whole new way of looking at life.

Copernicus and Galileo determined, in contrast to popular ideas and even to Greek teaching, that the earth goes around the sun rather than vice versa. The popular belief that the sun rises over the earth each morning was wrong. Instead, people learned that it is the earth's rotation that causes night and day.

For centuries many people had thought that heaven was a place somewhere above the earth. For faithful Christians it seemed rather nearby. Now, with the new information, it became harder to image the whereabouts of paradise. Isaac Newton's discoveries, well over a hundred years after Copernicus, added much more information to the nature of our world and the universe that ultimately changed the way literate people then and most people today think. In his book, Mathematical Principals of Natural Philosophy, written in 1687, he described how the earth and planets travel in orbits around the sun. He theorized that these movements were controlled by gravity, the enormous gravity of the sun holding all the planets in their circling orbits around it.

Newton couldn't explain gravity and what causes gravity remains a mystery even today. However, its effects helped to explain much of what was previously unknown. Basically, Newton showed that there was an order to life, to the movement of the earth and planets that operate along set rules and patterns. His discoveries may have led some notable men, including Thomas Jefferson and Benjamin Franklin, to become Deists. They believed that God had indeed created the universe but once he had set it in motion it proceeded without further need for his attention. Jefferson went so far as to make his own "Bible," which is basically a retelling of the New Testament with the removal of everything that Christ did of a miraculous nature.

The new science ushered in what was subsequently termed "The Age of Enlightenment." Philosophers and writers such as Jean-Jacques Rousseau, Voltaire, Immanuel Kant, John Locke, Adam Smith and Thomas Jefferson, believed in general that using reason mankind could understand the world and man's relationship to it. The allegiance people were previously thought to owe to the king and to the church was challenged leading to the bloody French Revolution of 1789 and to the doubts of many of the spiritual authority of both the Catholic and Protestant church. In the United States, the ideas of the Enlightenment helped to formulate the thinking of the founding fathers. They formally created the separation of the church and the state and also wrote guarantees of "life, liberty and pursuit of happiness" into the constitution. They also franchised voting rights to men who owned property. Much later in American history men without property, and later men of color and then finally women obtained the right to vote.

The great emphasis given by the Enlightenment to the power of human reason alone to make decisions and its weakening of the power of the king and the church led directly to the French Revolution and partially to the American Revolution. However, by the end of the French Revolution there was an abhorrence to the violence and a reaction to strict rationalism and a desire among many to return to an understanding that feelings and emotions are also important to people.

The Romantic Period ensued and it seemed to be in conflict with Enlightenment ideas. In reality it was a different way of looking at the world. We see the difference in approach in people today as well. Some maintain a very rationalistic and scientific view of life and the world while others see the world through their feelings, emotions and their intuitions. Neither of these two ways of looking at life is complete in itself. We are both rational beings and people with feelings and emotions. In general, the Romantic idealists felt that the Enlightenment ideas envisioned man as only a common entity rather than recognizing the individuality of each person.

Some major romantic literature of the period includes *The Scarlet Letter*, *Grimm's Fairy Tales* (think

Cinderella and Snow White, etc.), and the *Rime of the Ancient Mariner*, etc. A well-known Romantic novel that is long a part of our heritage is *Frankenstein*. Written in 1818 by Mary Shelley, its theme is basically a direct rebuke to the Enlightenment or Age of Reason. It's the story of a brilliant scientist who creates life from human body parts but is overwhelmed at the creature's ugliness. The creature, realizing he has been rejected both by his creator and then later by ordinary people, goes on a rampage of terror.

# Some Thoughts on Evolution

For thousands of years the account of God and the making of Adam and Eve was the belief of most people in the Christian, Jewish and Islamic world. Then along came Charles Darwin and his theory of evolution in 1859. The idea of evolution is certainly easy to understand. Its premise that all life started from a single cell which over eons of time evolved into the tremendous variety of life we see in the world today is classically simple. An initial difficulty with the theory is that to this day no one knows how life began. Darwin didn't, though he proposed the idea that life began in a primordial soup where dissolved chemicals chanced to come together to form life.

So far, scientists using the latest technology in trying to create life in the laboratory from non-life have not had any success. They have been able to utilize yeast cells and E. coli cells to make new combinations but that is making adjustments to things already living. So, for now, how life began on earth remains a mystery unless God had something to do with it.

One of the other unsolved problems in evolutionary theory was discovered in the middle of the last century. Watson, Crick, Wilkins and Franklin determined the amazingly complex structure of the DNA sequence that informs each cell in our body how to grow.

There are other questions about evolutionary theory that are hard to imagine such as the appearance of eyes and wings and the explosion of life in the Cambrian period. However, evolution is a simple, easy to understand theory that tries to connect all the dots. Things can and do evolve and the great variety of dogs may be an example. In the hundreds and thousands of years that man has owned dogs, huge varieties have interbred either on their own or with man's assistance resulting in the tiny Chihuahua breed to the huge English Mastiff that can weigh in excess of 300 pounds. All remain dogs, that is Canis Lupus, and can interbreed with each other and even with wolves which are also of the same species.

Darwin discovered varieties of finches of different size and bill shapes that recent findings show can also interbreed successfully. (From Evolution News, BBC News and other sources: Nature: Galapagos Finch "Species" can Interbreed. March 21, 2014) On the other hand, though horses and donkeys can mate with each other they are unable to transmit their genes further because their offspring, that is either a mule or a hinny, are infertile due to the difference in each parent animal's chromosomes. They are truly two different species of animals.

Evolution remains an influential and respected theory that tries to explain how life developed over billions of years from one celled creatures to the great variety of flora and fauna we have today. Was life unguided, completely by chance or "natural selection" as Darwin proposed or did God have a hand in guiding how life developed on earth? That is a subject for a later chapter.

# Seeing God in The Scientific Era of Today

We come now to the modern age, a time when change is happening at an even faster pace than before. Science is advancing to the point that we sometimes hope for new discoveries that can cure well known diseases, such as Alzheimer's and cancer. However, if such a cure is found, most people wouldn't call it a miracle but a scientific advancement. Nevertheless, the certainty that science can explain everything has taken a major downturn.

New scientific findings cast major doubts on what we can really know about life and the material world in which we live. In this chapter we will review some of these findings, many of which are not taught in primary or secondary schools. One is the discovery that the known universe was created at a specific point in time 13.8 billion years ago. Initially it was called with some derision the "Big Bang" and it is still known as that today. The time of the Big Bang has been scientifically determined and it is known and accepted by almost all scientists and yet no one can explain how it could have happened. For people of faith, not only those who are Christian, it is the work of God. It is how God created the universe which means that everything we know including the material of our bodies, the earth and the sun all result from God's creation.

What has furthermore been scientifically established is that even the material properties of our bodies and the matter making up our world was created long before the earth was formed. As the late Carl Sagan, astronomer and TV Cosmos series narrator famously said, "We are made of star stuff." That's because the carbon, oxygen and nitrogen in our world and our bodies as well as the iron in our blood was created in the intensely hot interior of former stars. It is evident to scientists that a great deal had to happen in advance over a period of billions of years to make a place for mankind to live and to create the elements necessary for human life as well as for all life.

Another major finding, as mentioned, is the discovery in the last century of DNA and its essential importance for life. Short for deoxyribonucleic acid, it is found in each cell and is the blueprint that guides each organism as it grows to follow the pattern of its kind. A stuff of amazing complexity found in each living cell, DNA is the essential material that guides the cells of each living thing to replicate true to its nature. Human beings, like all mammals, at the moment of conception have DNA in the sperm and the egg that guide the growth of cells to become a baby and then a man or a woman.

The tremendous complexity of the DNA in each living creature has been noted even by Bill Gates who remarked that "DNA is like a computer program but far, far more advanced than any software ever created." Our body type, the color of our eyes, our hair, skin, and if we will look something like our aunt, uncle, father or mother is all encoded in our DNA. Of course, there is no mention of DNA in the Bible and before the last century there was no scientific knowledge of it. However, as psalm 139, verses 13 and 14 describe: "For you created my inmost being; you knit me together in my mother's womb. I praise you because I am fearfully and wonderfully made."

For almost a hundred years scientists have tried to create life in the laboratory with no success. However, they have been able to make some changes to existing life and so, today, we have genetically modified food. And interestingly, thanks to scientific understanding of DNA, we can show how closely other creatures are related to human beings. To me, the findings are nothing short of amazing. As you might expect, primates, such as monkeys, gorillas and chimpanzees share up to 96 to 98 percent of human DNA. Surprisingly, even potatoes and bananas share 50% or more of human DNA. And mice and fruit flies share about 75% of our DNA. That is why they are frequently used in experiments for new medicine, etc. As for humans, no matter what race or ethnicity, we all share greater than 99.5 percent of the same DNA.

The next scientific finding can not only completely change the way we look at the world but can also show how God's hand keeps the world going. It's called quantum mechanics or quantum physics. The findings are nothing less than surprising and to some, including at first Albert Einstein, and hard to believe. Yet many of the benefits of the new science have already been utilized in our cell phones, computers, fiber optics, and laser scanners adding up our groceries and purchases as well as GPS so we can use our phones to confidently drive to places we've never been to before.

Quantum mechanics has to do with atoms, electrons and photons, the basic stuff that makes up all matter. We, and everything we see are made up of atoms. However, and though this is hard to understand, it has been proven in countless experiments, that the stuff of which we are made can exist both as particles and as waves. We think of ourselves and everything we see and touch as matter, much of it hard matter like a table, the walls, our house and automobiles. The reality is that if the electrons within the atoms stopped moving, everything would become so small as to be invisible. We, our house and that of our neighbors would all fit comfortably inside a thimble. That's because, as even Business Insider as well as scientific texts point out, 99.9999999 of our body is empty space and so is our house. It is the electrons traveling at huge relative distances to the nucleus and at a speed of almost five million miles per hour within each atom that accounts for our size and visibility. Scientists seem unable to explain how this is possible; for me it is God who keeps everything moving and in existence.

Then there are the all-important forces that science recognizes as governing every aspect of life and, in fact, the universe. They are named "the strong force," the "weak force," the "electromagnetic force" and gravity. I won't try to explain them here but scientists know that life could not exist on earth or anywhere in the universe without three of these forces acting within atoms. In actuality, it is known that without these very important forces of nature there would not be a universe at all! (BBC Science Focus Magazine November 2019, et al other scientific articles.) We might ask what caused these elementary forces to have the exact values necessary for life. Though they have been discovered within the lifetime of those of us who are older, information on how they came into existence and have their own specific values is not scientifically known.

The world of science is interesting and new discoveries are made all the time. Certainly, our material life is easier and far more comfortable than it was in the past. In many ways, even poor people today live much more comfortably than kings and queens in the past. Today, at least in industrialized countries, almost everyone has running water, comfortable beds and chairs, flush toilets and central heating. Science continues to expand our understanding of our universe and create medications that help in the fight against disease. It is not surprising that our lifespan is much longer now than in the Middle Ages or even one hundred years ago. The Social Security Act, for example, was enacted in 1935 when the average life expectancy for men in the United States was 61 and 65 for women. It's true that a few people then lived to be elderly. However, today great numbers of people routinely live into their seventies, eighties and nineties.

Science has reached the point where it can explain how many things occur but it is less able to explain why things happen. There remains so much to be learned but, in many ways, we are only scratching the surface of all that can be known. Here are three examples. Gravity is a huge force that affects us and the universe but we don't know what gravity is. Another unknown is the mysterious "dark matter" and "dark energy" that permeate our universe and remains an unknown even though scientists say that together they constitute 95% of the cosmos. That leaves the known universe—stars, galaxies, our solar system etc. constituting only 5% of what we can visualize and look at with our telescopes. On a more human level, one that affects tens of millions of people, science still doesn't know what it is that causes Alzheimer's disease, migraine headaches, autism or Parkinson's disease.

Modern science does a good job of measuring things. With powerful microscopes we can measure the size of tiny microbes and even viruses. We also know the size of the earth and moon and the distance in light years to the nearest stars and farthest galaxies that can be observed with our advanced telescopes. However, on the human level, scientists have no instruments to measure love, hate or any other feelings or sentiments that mean so much to us. Because they cannot be weighed or measured, science can tell us nothing about God, angels or the soul or spirit of human beings. All these are outside the grasp of science.

# A Beautiful but not Perfect World

There is no doubt that we live in a beautiful world. The wonderful expanses of our natural parks, the great lakes, the views of the mountains, snowcapped in winter, are inspiring and cause us to take pause. When we get away from the lights of the city and into the country, we can be truly amazed at the beauty of the skies lit by the stars, the moon, the planets and the milky way. Similarly, the power and the beauty of the oceans, lakes and streams can be stunning and are the inspiration for countless paintings done in appreciation of their natural splendor.

Of course, not all is perfect. The gardener and the farmer are quite aware of the weeds that continuously crop up unbidden. The hiker or anyone going on a woodsy trail knows to stay away from the three leaved poison ivy and the creeping brambles with sharp thorns. For those who read the Bible, the third chapter of Genesis describes how the soil will be “accursed” because of the sin of Adam and Eve and “It will yield you brambles and thistles, as you eat the produce of the land.”

Nevertheless, in general our world, the third from the sun, is the only place we know of where humans can live in relative comfort. Our atmosphere is breathable, conducive to life and our temperatures, except in Northern climes, are comfortable bordering on warm during the day if one needs to be out in the sun. For tens of thousands of years, the trees which grow naturally in most regions of the world have supplied the firewood used in fire pits and fireplaces to keep mankind warm and to cook our food. Likewise, these often beautiful trees provide shade in the hot summer months and let the light of the sun through for warmth during the colder months of the year. Similarly, rain falls naturally in season, with some exceptions, to provide adequate moisture to grow our crops. In many drier areas of the world people have for thousands of years successfully channeled rivers like the Nile and the Euphrates and many others into canals to irrigate the surrounding countryside.

Water is, as it turns out, is a most unusual substance but vital to us and for life on earth. Our bodies are made up of about 70% water and the blood that circulates within us is mostly water. The unique fact that water on freezing is less dense than liquid water allows it to not only float atop our water and soft drinks but also to float on our lakes and streams. If it didn't float, fish and aquatic life would be crushed beneath the ice and the earth would be plunged into a permanent and severe ice age.

Besides the beauty of the world, we have others things to please us. Our home, furnished in the style we like, is often our place of comfort and refuge from all the goings on of the world. A dog or a cat can become almost extensions of our families and they give us immense enjoyment. Dogs follow our lead and really miss us when we're gone. They are loving creatures. Cats often have a mind of their own but they're cute, cuddly creatures that love to snuggle with their owners. Even the birds that come to our bird feeder, if we have one, are fun to watch as they grab a seed and fly away or hungrily stay for a meal.

I don't think we can leave this section without mentioning the beauty and the power of human love. We grow up in families where, if we're fortunate, we are loved. Most of us love our mother and father and even our grandparents. Then, when we reach maturity the great majority of us seek out someone with whom we can bond. When we find him or her, we are happy. The happiness we feel may last months, years or a lifetime. It's a great comfort to live life with someone who knows us intimately, who loves us well and who, despite the inevitable occasional disagreements and misunderstandings, really cares about us.

# Suffering

Why would a good God allow so much suffering and evil? We see it all around us in far off places and near, the killings, disease and natural disasters, and the heartfelt sorrow that affects us personally when a major sickness or death strikes those we love.

Our faith in God can be shaken when personal tragedy strikes home with debilitating illness, incurable cancer or Alzheimer's afflicts us personally or someone we love. We might even ask God, "Lord why did you allow this? Is this how you treat someone who has been a faithful follower?"

In the midst of suffering in our better moments we may realize that Christ suffered also in his terrible death on the cross. However, that may not diminish our feeling that we live in a deplorable world with far too much evil and tragedy. If God is good, why didn't he make the world a better place? There are at least two answers to the question. The first we know already—the fall caused by the sin of Adam and Eve that extends to all mankind. This Bible verse describes it well: "By the sweat of your face will you earn your food, until you return to the ground, as you were taken from it. For dust you are and to dust you shall return." Genesis, 3:19.

The second answer has to do with our freedom. Yes, God could have made it impossible for anyone to sin thus preventing anyone from committing murder, from rape, lying, cheating, yelling at someone, or even drinking too much, gossiping, telling white lies, etc. If God took away our freedom to sin it would make parenting easier, preventing children from disobeying, sassing or making fun of their parents. Of course, such a world would not be the real world we know today. Evil would not be present and people would not be free to make other than good choices. We would have no other choice but to be always good. Consequently, our love for God and for friends and family would be automatic as we would have no other option.

In sum, if God did not permit us to sin, we would be nothing more than automatons. We would be programmed only to do good. That is not what God wants for us. He wants us to have freedom in our daily personal lives. He gives us free choice, that is to either love Him or to turn away. No one is forced to love God. That includes the angels. Being spirits and far more knowledgeable than us they were given only one unalterable choice. To love God or to turn away. Those that turned from God are devils. They seek to ensnare others and to make them like themselves. That's another reason why there is evil in the world. With the devil's prompting or on their own people can turn away from God and can also turn against the people that God created. We are aware that there are people who only care for themselves. They use other people to get what they want. They can be kind if it helps them to advance their own interests or they can be evil and vindictive especially when they don't get what they want.

We human beings live in a complex world with a great number of temptations. We want to be loved but are often prompted to love ourselves first and foremost. God knows our weaknesses. He knows how often we struggle to do the right thing. God knows that each of us is subject to temptations. Even when on earth and the woman caught in adultery was brought before him his will was to not hold her to the Jewish law of stoning an adulteress. He said to those who were accusing her, "Let the one among you who is without sin be the first to throw a stone at her." (John 8:6) Jesus knew then and now that no one is free from sin. In the case of the woman, after the others had walked away, he told her,

“Neither do I condemn you. Now go and sin no more.” Though we are all sinners, it is God’s will that we seek His aid to overcome temptations. Even though many turn away from God there is always a chance and a hope that they will turn back to Him. God is patient, ever loving, and solicitous that each individual finds his or her way back into His graces.

# Religion in The Age of Today

The 21st century has brought great changes to life, many of which affect religious belief and participation. Certainly, it is true that almost everyone is on the internet today either via computer or in any event through cellphone. That fact alone alters the social landscape and can definitely affect our view of religion. In addition, people in the Western world, that is mainly the United States and Europe, have inherited particular mindsets or ways at looking at things that differentiates our view from the people of Asia, Africa and China. It should be no surprise that Eastern thinking is very different from Western thinking.

The way we look at life as well as religion is greatly influenced by the Enlightenment, by science, by modernism and by post modernism. We look to science to bring continuing improvements to our lives in medicine, in comfort and in our standard of living. In many ways this has happened although more recently we have seen a downturn in our lifespan in the United States. On average, Americans don't live quite as long as Europeans.

Historically, the prevailing view of people of the West was shaped by the Bible and Christianity. The words Jesus spoke about love of neighbor, forgiveness and his death on the cross and resurrection are paramount for his followers. Until modern times the ordinary person on the street believed that God created the world as was told in Genesis and that God actively cares for the earth and mankind. The Enlightenment led some people to come to a different understanding. The new astronomical discoveries of the time showed not only that the earth is only one of many bodies that orbit the sun, but also revealed that the earth and all the planets are kept in place by a force called gravity rather than by the hand of God. Of course, it can just as well be said that gravity is one of the important ways that God keeps the solar system as well as the universe in order.

As mentioned, no one then or today really knows what causes gravity. It remains a mystery though some scientists have proposed that it is gravitons that cause large objects to attract each other even at great distances. However, thus far scientists have not been able to detect gravitons. For now, all we can do is have some understanding of how gravity works. Nevertheless, the idea that man could begin to comprehend the laws of nature gave impetus for thoughtful people to utilize this understanding in many areas that have led to invention, innovation and the industrial revolution.

Today, we are the inheritors of scientific thinking that permeates how we look at everything including our faith. The fact that we tend to view things from a Western rather than an Eastern mindset is a given for people raised in Europe and the United States. It may be one reason why in general Christianity is growing more slowly in the West than in the East. However, it may not be so much that our Western thinking has changed as that other factors are affecting us. After all, fifty years ago most Americans went to church regularly. The real revolution has happened within our own personal lives. For many, the internet and social media have changed the way we interact with our friends and the world.

There are many good things to note about the internet to go along with those that are not so good. The internet allowed many of us to work from home during Covid 19 and children could likewise attend school via the internet. The major change that affects almost all of us has happened because of cellphones and social media. It would not be an exaggeration to say that in two decades the internet has changed the way we live. Unfortunately, it has not been all for the better.

Today, most of us don't want to leave home without our phone. And also today, many of us, including teens and preteens, are connected to various social media sites including Facebook, Instagram, Snapchat and TikTok to name a few. These sites can become addictive perhaps because some of our friends are on them and who would want to miss a message from a friend? For teens, and young people, some just entering the world of social life, connecting on the phone can become addictive. Teens and youth so much want to fit in that they can easily spend the greater part of their free time hooked on using their cell phones. They don't want to miss out on anything. This may be one factor in why many young people don't go to church.

It is not just young people who are affected. Great numbers of older people also want to be online especially with the popularity and easy access of internet sites beginning with Facebook (Meta) which began not so long ago in 2004. Of course, these media sites are also replete with ever present advertising. It's to be expected that people often like to add their own personal thoughts on these sites. However, their political opinions and thoughts on other matters may be agreeable or disagreeable to you. Unfortunately, inflammatory, divisive, and even discriminatory language on social medium sites is not at all unusual. And it is all too easy to get worked up and respond in kind to offensive language.

As unsettling as media sites can be, they may also be used carefully and well to keep in contact with family and friends who may be geographically distant. Limiting the access to our personal media sites for people who are inflammatory, make untrue and inappropriate statements is important for our peace of mind and our sanity. No one should have to be riled up because they want to keep in touch with others and sometimes it may be necessary to drop a "friend" who is insulting or abusive.

Time spent on media can keep people from church but there is a darker side of the internet that may be having even more of a negative effect on church attendance—internet porn. Internet porn can and does affect people of all ages from preteens to the elderly. In fact, if the reporting on the subject is correct, most men and a large percentage of women view internet porn at least on occasion. It is reported that even some youth ministers and pastors watch it online.

What is especially tragic is that pornography can pop up unbidden and unwanted at any time. Unfortunately, it has become almost ubiquitous. Before the growth of porn there were always "girly magazines" but they were often placed in a rack secure in the back part of a store with a sign saying you must be 18 to look at those mags. Nowadays porn can and does pop up on the screens of preteens and those even younger. Sex has always been alluring for almost everyone but especially for young teens and young men. Porn sites are a multi-billion-dollar industry and in doing the research for this book it is apparently indisputable that many men and teens spend excessive hours a week intently watching.

What are some of the outcomes of those who watch excessive porn. Surveys show that loneliness, estrangement from religious practice and marital infidelity leading frequently to marital breakup are some of the outcomes. Erectile dysfunction is also linked to excessive porn consumption. It is truly unfortunate that along with the internet porn is so readily available.

Long ago, a man looked down from his parapet and saw a woman bathing. He wanted her. The man was King David, the most beloved of all the kings of Israel. Though the woman was married, how could Bathsheba refuse her handsome and powerful king? A child was conceived from their union so something had to be done. David knew what to do; he put her husband, Uriah, in the forefront of the lines of battle. He died there, fighting for his king. Not until later did David realize the full sinfulness of what he had done. In fact, we are told it grieved him for the rest of his life. Seventy-three are the number of the psalms in the Bible attributed to David. Number 51 is the one that expresses his great sorrow.

# Social Media: Positives and Negatives

Social media sites like Facebook, Twitter and a host of others in general started off well, offering us good and speedy ways to communicate and connect with others. They are used by many if not most Americans and people of other countries to help us keep in touch with friends and relatives. As mentioned, Facebook got its start in 2004 and Twitter in 2006. Instagram launched in 2010, TikTok in 2016. Snapchat, LinkedIn, and of course YouTube are a few of the wildly popular sites for social interaction among other newer sites. These sites are basically free to users and have the great advantage of immediacy that far surpasses sending a card or letter. Though the sites are free to users they are not free to businesses that utilize social media sites to advertise their products and services. Companies are content to pay the cost of advertising. Their professionals design ads they know will appeal to a wide range of people. Many sites are huge moneymakers for their founders and generate from thousands to billions of dollars.

The companies using social media, both small and large, are able to increase their revenue by regularly adding advertising on media sites. Moreover, most sites have systems in place to monitor individual users for their preferences so that companies can target their advertising to appeal to what is most likely to attract a person's interest or attention. That is why if you buy something, or even spend time looking at a product online, you will soon see more of the same or similar products appear when you are using your phone or computer. Before long, Facebook and other media sites get to know a great deal about us and our personal preferences.

The goal of most if not all popular media sites is to get us to stay on the app as long as possible. In that way they can increase their revenue from their advertisers who pay according to how often their advertisements are viewed. At the same time, social media sites use attractive layouts and interactive features designed to pique one's interest and keep one scrolling or clicking to get more information or more likes. All the while, more advertising is displayed with the hope that something will have immediate or delayed interest for us.

That was the pattern that played out on most media sites until more recent years. Since then, starting in 2009, a more dangerous and dramatic development has changed media and distressed many users. In that year Facebook gave users a way to publicly "like" posts. Twitter did something similar but even more powerful that same year when it allowed users to "Retweet" posts thus sharing it with all their followers. Facebook followed with its "Share" button which likewise posted content to followers.

Soon, some of the users of the media sites realized that if they could come up with content or posts of a unique or provocative nature they might suddenly "go viral" and thus obtain sudden internet fame. Unfortunately, it didn't seem to matter if the content was actually true or not. What subsequently happened then is that some users posted "news" that attracted attention because of its shocking nature even though the content was not necessarily true.

Facebook and Twitter learned that what really grabs people's attention is shocking or emotion laden content often directed at opposition groups. This phenomenon has become especially apparent during the run up to elections in American politics. Unfortunately, free speech, even when it is actually outright lies, is protected by the constitution such that what one politician, or anyone for that matter, says about another may be completely untrue or untrue in context.

Media giants don't ordinarily support one candidate over another. However, they know that in generating and elevating controversy through their algorithms they keep users on their sites for longer times and thus generate more revenue because of more exposure to ads.

Moreover, and this is important to note, what one person receives when accessing Facebook, Twitter or other sites is likely to be very different from that of someone else. That's because the media giants through their algorithms analyze what most turns on each individual user so that they can feed you more of what most interests you. That way you will stay tuned in longer to the app and see more advertising.

A person who is on Facebook or other media site to connect with friends and who does not get involved in controversy will see a much tamer Facebook account than others who engage in confrontation. Moreover, a person who in normal society is a real outlier, a loner, one who for example expresses a desire to kill an elected official or someone else will be able to link up with others who have similar inclinations. They can then communicate with each other and even make plans to work together. That is a major danger of social media; that people whose ideas are far out there can unite and even act together in nefarious schemes. It is a primary reason why today elected officials and others receive death threats from anonymous sources, often from people who have become riled up by social media.

Social media sites will tend to give you what you want in order that you will spend more time using the site. If you tend to believe in conspiracy theories and indicate that preference on social media you will soon be inundated with more of the same. If you tend toward gullibility all kinds of things can be made to seem believable.

In general, regardless of social media, we have our own lives to live. We make choices that affect us and those we love. Having hobbies or interests aside from media is healthy and helps to keep us grounded in the real world of day to day living. Getting some exercise is probably important for everyone. In reality, there's little most of us can do to affect what goes on in the world, but we can do much to improve things at home with family and friends. Let's start there, spending time where we can have a real impact on making our world and that of others better and friendlier.

# Protecting Children: Then, and in Today's World

Does the age of the internet and social media affect children? Do we need to be more concerned for our youth today? We all want the best for our children. Back in the middle of the last century people didn't seem to worry as much about them being safe. As a child during that time, I enjoyed playing at the vacant yard next to our house which was overgrown with weeds, small trees and all kinds of insects. By nine years old I had a paper route and each week collected the 35 or 45 cents from every customer except those always in arrears or hard to find at home.

I loved the outdoors and by nine my parents also let me travel along the nearby creek which led in a mile to Garfield Park. The creek had some small fish, plenty of turtles and was always interesting to me whether a slow moving stream or a gushing river. I'd meet boys I knew, some from the other richer side of the creek and one of them introduced me to cigarette smoking at the age of ten. Of course, I didn't tell my parents about that.

As for safety, I was glad at only nine years old to have passed the swimming test allowing me to swim in the deep water and jump off the ten foot diving board. However, when someone jumped on top of me while swimming, I realized the need to be careful. Then, even more dangerous, as I rode my bicycle home one day from the park, I was hit by a car. The car and I were both making a right hand turn onto the boulevard and the vehicle turned too sharply, sideswiping me. Fortunately, the place I landed was grassy and I wasn't hurt. Having paper route money, I replaced the damaged bike fender and the other with brand new chrome fenders. They looked great! However, someone else also liked them and before long my bicycle was stolen. Lesson learned about making things too attractive. I also had a bad encounter with four boys on bicycles close to my own neighborhood. They called themselves "The Ringgold Gang," the name of a local street, and they roughed me up mainly by hitting me in the stomach. I was never so scared, but they finally let me go.

My experience with bullying in school was partly my own fault. The first that I remember occurred in third grade with a boy who got into the habit of saying mean things to me as I walked on my way home from school. One day we fought, tumbling to the ground as we tried to pummel each other. Maybe I had the upper hand as afterword he never said another thing against me. The next time was in the schoolyard with a new kid who some of us played tag football with. He had a rough way about him and I said things against him until one day he fought me, teaching me not to do that. Then, in a later grade there was a new black kid in class who was placed in the seat in front of mine. He seemed to me to be smart as well as extremely confident such that I chided him frequently until he took it out on me in the restroom. That kid was strong! What I personally learned however is that kids, at least through sixth grade, can't really hit each other hard enough to do real damage.

My last fight was in high school with a friend. By that time, I had gained some size. We were walking by the creek on a warm muggy day and had been, for whatever reason, sniping verbally at each other. Then, it turned to fists. We each got in a good hit to the face. Then we immediately stopped. I think we both realized we could seriously hurt each other or knock out a tooth if we continued.

As for an encounter with a sexual predator, that came when I was close to thirteen. Collecting money on my paper route, there was a man who always seemed friendly in an almost joking way when I appeared at his door. One day he invited me inside supposedly to show me something. So, we sat on the edge of his bed and I soon realized he wanted me to show him my masculinity. I resisted and started to get up to leave when he physically restrained me, arm around my shoulder, holding me back. I was not a big kid then, only five feet two, and he was a fairly large guy. Nevertheless, by standing up quickly and pushing forward I was able to get out of his grasp and rush to the door. Needless to say, I never went into that house again.

Today, our children may encounter some of the same kinds of things but maybe in a different way. We may not be as willing to let our children roam as freely as back then. I think we have a heightened sense of danger because of our news and media outlets. Even our local newspaper seems to highlight crime in the first few pages.

In actuality, from crime statistics over the years, the fifties and sixties were good years with low homicide rates nationally. Then came the more crime filled seventies, eighties and nineties with at times as much as double the earlier homicide rates. Then, the rates went significantly down again between the years 2000 to 2018, only to go up during the pandemic years, but not as high as in the eighties and nineties. Data is still incomplete, but there are some indications, the Chicago homicide rate for example, that since the height of the pandemic, murder rates appear to be going down again. (Most data cited here is from the FBI Uniform Crime Reports)

I know that with our own children, at young ages our sons were often gone most of the day in the summer and on weekends to different places where they would frequently meet their friends. With our girls, it was different. Just recently, I was walking with my daughter-in-law in an area on the other side of the train tracks where the only footprints in the light snow were those of deer and rabbits. There was a small forest to the right of us and she told me that as a woman she would never feel safe to walk in such a secluded area. I walk there on occasion, usually carrying a cane or walking stick to beat back the brambles, but she made me realize that I wouldn't want one of my daughters going there alone.

Early on, we need to set limits with our children. To stay away from a hot oven is one of the first things to learn as toddlers and to be careful on stairs is another. Recently our youngest grandson jumped down a number of stairs and ended up having to wear a foot cast for several weeks. Fortunately, no surgery was needed. The outdoors can multiply dangers, especially where there is street traffic. Children need to have an awe of vehicles and should not be allowed to cross any street themselves until they are older and have been carefully taught to look both ways. Before that they need to be holding the hand of an adult. I was appalled and upset not too long ago when I saw a young girl dash out ahead of her mother into a busy intersection. The light was green for the traffic and there was a bus and a car coming down the street. Fortunately, the vehicle rushing toward her was able to stop in time. It could have been so terrible!

The internet makes child rearing more complicated for parents. Few parents today grew up with the easy accessibility of the entire spectrum of cyberspace on our cell phones. Long before the internet, there was television which has been around for ages. Some parents have made the mistake of allowing children to spend long hours in front of the screen as a kind of babysitter to keep them quiet. Research shows the practice is not healthy at all for children under 18 months and it is known that violent TV content can cause fears and sleeplessness even in older children.

The danger to children (as well as some adults) brought by the internet is twofold. Let's discuss them one at a time. The first is gaming. The makers of popular video games spend much money and time to make them as exciting and as addictive as possible. They want their users to continue to play and play and play and to tell others about how exciting the games are. The mistake some parents can make in providing the games and the devices with which to play them is in thinking that spending hours playing a game is completely harmless fun. Some parents are so worried about danger outdoors that they feel that their children are safer inside. It is true that there are some limited areas within large cities where there is more danger. However, when a child is so hooked on video games that he or she can't sleep and doesn't care much about eating, it's time for parents to take action. Also, when children don't do their homework or don't want to go to school or have any interest in socializing with friends, it is long past time to limit their playing of video games.

Cell phones have become endemic in our culture. Few today want to leave home without their phone. What if something happened? Our perceived need for cell phones soon extends to providing them for our children so they can stay connected. But, as we know, a cell phone does much more than place and receive calls. In reality it is a small computer able to access the whole world of media. Almost anything out there can be obtained with a cell phone including music, interaction with friends, news, video games and pornography. It is clear that some sites can be harmful to children.

Today, especially because of the very real danger that children and youth can get a warped view of sexuality through pornography, it is important for parents to talk to their children at an early age. Letting them know that the parts of the body covered by bathing suits should not be exposed in graphic imagery is a start when they are young. It is important to be comforting, not alarmist with children of any age, for today, no matter how well you protect and monitor phones and computer, it is almost inevitable that they will happen on some pornography at home or on the phone of a school friend. Ideally, your children should feel open enough in their relationship with you to talk with you about it. Let them know that sex is a good thing, that it is how children like themselves are conceived and come into the world. Let them know that porn sex is an exaggeration of the real sex experienced when a couple is in love with each other. Porn is not reality.

If, however, you learn that your child, despite any parental control programs you may have installed, is hooked on porn, it is time to take action. This is especially the case when their grades at school are falling and they are no longer interested in socializing with friends. At that point it is time to sit down and talk about the situation and it may also be time to monitor their computer usage and limit screen time and cell phone hours.

Unfortunately, there is another hazard that comes with the internet. We've mentioned it in the preceding chapter, but especially with teens there are more specific dangers. Teens, like adults, use their phones much more than simply to make calls. They text messages, use different media sites such as Snapchat, TikTok, YouTube, Instagram, etc. Many like to be tuned in to music or play video games while at other times they may look up information. Probably most teens turn to their phones when they're bored or when for whatever reason they have to wait.

Unfortunately, some teens can become so preoccupied with social media that they feel they must at all times be ready to answer a text, chat, or respond to an incoming message. They may even text while driving, obviously very dangerous, or answer late night posts rather than sleep. Often teens have a fear that they will miss something. What may be worse for them is to see a photo or video of their friends enjoying time together and they are left out.

Some teens, like some adults, feel they need to be in on everything. It can become a major concern for them when someone transmits a disparaging remark or even an inappropriate photo. Cyberbullying may be ignored if it is a onetime event but should be reported if it becomes a continuing pattern. The teen years are a time to grow, to learn, and to become fully capable adults ready to take their place in the world. Like any time of life, it does have its ups and downs and times when teens may need to lean on others for support. It's human for all of us at such a time to seek the help of someone we trust.

# A New Beginning

Those of us who are older and more or less faithful Christians might appreciate a return to packed churches where we saw many of our friends and their children. Would Jesus Christ be happy at that? Yes, if all those in the pews were faith-filled Christians. However, Jesus does ask something of those who choose to follow him. From His perspective, attendance at church services alone may not be sufficient.

First of all, it is clear that Jesus does welcome sinners. He knows we are all imperfect beings and because we are human, we often have trouble doing the right thing. The Pharisees had a problem with Christ's love for sinners. They asked his disciples, "Why does he eat with tax collectors and sinners?" (Matt 9:11) Jesus extended his love to those not acceptable to the

Pharisees as well as to the poor woman caught in adultery. It should be clear that we are all welcome in Jesus' eyes no matter what we have done as long as we return to him with sincere regret for our failings.

Jesus did have a problem with self-righteous people, who in his time included most of the Pharisees. The Pharisees looked at religion in a different way than the majority of people do today. They believed that the way to salvation was to be observant in following all the religious laws. However, the majority of them seemed lacking in their love of God and concern for God's people. Jesus expressed their condition well with this quite explicit parable: 'Two man went up to the temple to pray, one a Pharisee, the other a tax collector. The Pharisee stood there and said this prayer to himself, "I thank you, God, that I am not grasping, unjust, adulterous like everyone else, and particularly that I am not like this tax collector here. I fast twice a week; I pay tithes on all I get." The tax collector stood some distance away, not daring even to raise his eyes to heaven; but he beat his breast and said, "God be merciful to me, a sinner." This man, I tell you, went home justified; the other did not. For everyone who raises himself up will be humbled, but anyone who humbles himself will be raised up.' (Luke 18:10-14) It is apparent from this that Jesus has no fondness for the prideful man or woman who is so much into themselves that they forget to be thankful for the gifts God has given them.

There are a multitude of reasons why people don't attend services as much as in the past. As mentioned, hours spent on the internet leaves less time. Others, including some who spend time on internet porn, and others who are "living in sin" (whatever that might mean) may not feel that they would be welcome inside a church. However, the Christ who "eats with sinners" welcomes us to return to his love.

Then there are the Christians who may have been attending but have been turned off by something the priest or minister said. This seems to happen a lot. What I believe these people forget is that they can and probably should stand up for their own beliefs. Not that they should directly confront the minister, who after all is human and also makes mistakes. No, the relationship each one of us has with God is personal. God loves each one of us for ourselves and though we may be part of a particular church God speaks to us individually. Speaking personally, my wife and I have definitely taken issue at times with something said by the minister at the podium. We are not going to leave our church and the friends we have made because of an issue with which we are not in agreement. However, it is understandable that a particular church or minister may have an agenda that you just can't live with. In that case, it may be time to move on, not drop out.

Then, there is a large group of Christians who say "I GET NOTHING OUT OF IT." Excuse my gut response, do you put anything into it? The standard and true response is WE ARE THE CHURCH. The church is not really the building at all but you and me. Without us the church building is nothing but an empty shell. It is the people inside adding their prayers and their singing voices giving praise to God that is the church. Yes, it's true, if you take a seat near the back, don't listen and don't pray you're likely to get nothing out of church. It's the **participation** that matters and the giving thanks to God who made each one of us and cares for each of us.

Yes, God loves you and me and each of us personally but He never has and never will force us to worship Him. So, if you have a friend who says he or she gets nothing out of the service, try asking them to participate at church. Maybe they will say they don't have a singing voice; might they try to quietly hum along? Certainly, they can voice their amen and respond as best they can to prayers and petitions. You might offer to attend church with them, including them alongside your family if you attend together. People do at times need encouragement and you can help them to see what they are missing.

Besides all the time many spend on social media, there is another relatively new factor affecting church participation. As our society has become more secular, we find more activities and sports scheduled for Sunday mornings, which for Christians is the traditional time for church. How difficult it must be for faith-filled parents to miss a service because of scheduled game times. Fortunately, at least in most Catholic churches, there are Saturday evening masses and a few even have Sunday evening services. Some Protestant churches also have evening services on weekdays. We want our children to be able to participate and compete and so it may be necessary to make other arrangements. Attending church on another day besides Sunday may be an alternative possibility for some. The important thing is to take time for God even if at times we cannot strictly follow the ordinary schedule. Some services are broadcast on TV which is great for those who are ill though it is not the same as personal attendance at a church. At the very least, and I would not advocate it generally, take time with your children and your family for an in-home prayer service where you select readings and prayers to keep in personal touch with God our creator.

Jesus wants our love. But Jesus as well as God the Father want to be loved **first**. That means to be loved above all people and things of the world. That is the hard part for us. We human beings can become so easily distracted and often tend to hold other things in higher regard. For some, the pursuit of money can easily become a god in their lives. That is, the thing that a person strives for more than anything else including God. It is easy for a person to feel they're doing right by their family in spending long hours earning a big income. However, if one is never there with their own family because of work, one's absence will be missed to say the least. Children do best with both a mother and father actively in the picture. Many other things can be given first importance before God. For example, a substance addiction, a lover or even the pursuit of fame can easily become more important to an individual than God.

Addictions of any kind, including those just mentioned, are normally not easy to overcome. Reaching out to God, to the Blessed Virgin Mary or the saints, and to others who can help is the beginning of controlling these strongly felt desires. Ultimately, overcoming long held desires and habits will often take time but ours is a God ready to forgive each time we fall for as long as it takes. God doesn't ever give up on us, but we sometimes give up on ourselves. The turning point for us as individuals is recognizing God's deep love for each of us and acknowledging it by taking steps to turn toward Him in our day to day lives.

# On Living the Good Life

Everyone would like to live the “good life” but for many the popular idea of doing so is having a lot of money and living a glamorous and expensive life style. However, even secular articles appearing in magazines and psychological publications are quite clear that money is not really a major factor in living the good life. We obviously need money in order to live and conduct our affairs. However, other things like friendships, a sense of purpose, being kind, being self-confident, healthy eating, setting goals, learning to forgive, learning to say no are other important aspects to living a good life. Other things such as having a hobby, taking time for light or rigorous exercise, learning generosity and to count our blessings are more ideas that are frequently mentioned in articles and books on how to find happiness in life.

The good life can be embraced by many if not by most people today including those not affiliated with a particular faith. Is life different if one is a Christian? Many surveys indicate that people who attend religious services, whether they be Protestant, Catholic, Islamic, Jewish or other tend in general to be happier than those who don't. (Pew Research January 31, 2019: Religions Relationship to Happiness, Civic Engagement and Health Around the World et al.) Surveys show that those who go to church also tend to be somewhat more active in voluntary organizations and are more likely than others to vote in elections. Also, as reported by Time Magazine and others, they tend to live longer than the unchurched. One Ohio State University study shows that people who attend religious services live on average four years longer.

Like all human beings, Christians experience many of the same joys, concerns and problems. No one, even the rich and famous, is able to escape the downturns in life that happens when a family member dies, when a friendship is broken or a love affair ends. Many of us may also experience severe financial concerns at one point or another in our lives. Advertising encourages us to buy big pickups, expensive cars and fine houses. Usually, we don't need the added expense but we like the macho image of the big truck or the upscale vehicle with all the extra features.

Unfortunately, an unexpected major illness, loss of employment, a major car problem or even the need for a new roof can set us back and create stress in our lives. Then there are the almost to be expected multiplying health problems that come especially as we grow older. That part of life is little different for the atheist or for the Christian. The difference really has to do with our outlook and with one special relationship.

For those of us who are Christians, our belief is that God created the universe, the world and all the good things and people found on earth. We believe that we are "made in the "image of God," as is stated in the first book of the Bible. We are given intelligence, far more than any animal, and can remember our past and make plans for the future.

A Christian doesn't expect life to be a bed of roses; Jesus never promised that. However, a believer feels in their heart and mind that God cares what happens to him or her and is there to support us during difficult times. A Christian has such a relationship with God that he or she can call on Him in tough times and be answered. A believer doesn't have to go through everything alone but is lifted up by the felt personal support of a loving God. A Christian talks to God during difficult times and in good times. God is there for him or her.

When things are going well, a Christian is thankful. This appreciation extends to giving thanks for a good meal, for good personal relationships, and even for good weather. He or she is appreciative of all that God gives in this beautiful world.

So, in reality, a believer doesn't live alone even if they do in fact live alone in the common sense of the word. God is with him or her in all their waking hours and even when they lie down to sleep or awaken in the morning. A believer feels the presence of God during many hours of the day. It's a comforting feeling to know that someone loves us, especially during those times when we may feel that the world doesn't very much love or appreciate us.

How do we explain the source of our joy to those who lack faith? They also need to trust that there is Someone who cares for them. In order to do so they need to turn toward God, and to turn away from their pride and sinful desires that are not in accord with the Lord's teachings. In sum, they need to ask for forgiveness so they can turn toward God. Jesus wants the love of each person for he said, "I am the way the truth and the light. No one comes to the Father except through me." (John 14:6) And yet, as mentioned, we only need to begin to turn to Him and He will help us along the rest of the way. He will never give up on us.

Do those of us who are Christian have a part in the lives of those who are not? Yes, though we might prefer that they join us but that doesn't always happen. Each person makes their own way in life and in faith. And yet the Reverend Ronald Rolheiser, author of numerous books and a columnist in approximately 90 publications makes the point that "our faith already baptizes those we love." He goes on to say, "Thanks to the marvels of the Incarnation, every sincere Christian can say 'My heaven includes this or that particular person whom I love.'"

In his column, Reverend Rolheiser makes the point that "God loves these persons more than we do and is more solicitous for their happiness and salvation than we are." Rolheiser compares God's love and patience with men and women to a GPS that is always giving us directions. If we make a wrong turn in life, He is constantly giving us new directions to reroute us back to Him. Rolheiser says definitively that despite the number of times we go in the wrong direction God never gives up on us

I am rereading the book by St. Therese of Lisieux, the Little Flower, titled *The Story of a Soul*. She was such an unusual child who, at a young age, told both her mother and father she wished they were dead. Strange, isn't it? Her thinking was that if they died, they would immediately receive the joy of heaven. I think that as Christians we all believe in paradise though we may not be in any hurry to get there. Personally, I believe that life on earth is generally good but heaven will be much better. What I do think and hope we might be able to emulate are Therese's last words uttered seconds before she died at only twenty-four. "Oh! I love Him! . . . My God. . .I love You!"

I have witnessed death, the death of a man strong in his faith. As he lay on his bed in our house, my wife and her sister sang religiously inspired songs as he was dying. Then, an amazing thing happened. As he took his last breath, a huge wide smile came over his face. Though I had known him for many years, I had never seen such a great smile. The three of us looked at each other. Of course, there was sadness, for he was my wife and her sister's father, but we knew he had passed on to a far better place.

## God's Relationship with Us

If like most people, we believe that God had something to do with creating the universe, our world, and the great variety of life we see around us, a question may remain for some. Is God an aloof God who had something to do with creation but then leaves everything to develop on its own, or does He really care about people, who from our point of view, are His finest creation? Many would answer that question in one sentence. He cares about us. We may have that intuitive feeling, one that is backed up by what we know of both the Old and New Testament. But why? Why does the all-powerful God care about people?

People much smarter than me have reached important conclusions about the nature of God that may answer the question. It starts with the Trinity, a central tenet of belief in all faiths that call themselves Christian. It is the belief in three persons in one God. The recognition of this is found sprinkled almost innumerable times in both the Old and New Testament. What this means is that God is not lonely, not a single though powerful being who exists before all time. What seems to be true is that from all time God has been a relational being. In scripture, the love of God the Father for the Son and vice versa is clear. Also, the love of the third person, the Holy Spirit, is evident. Thus, from before all time, God the Father, the Son and the Holy Spirit have been a loving threesome. This has major implications for us. Why did God create the universe and Adam and Eve? It was not because God was lonely. God is happy. In his creativity He made the universe and all that is in it. God has no need for human beings to bring anything to His existence. No, it would appear that as a loving being, God created human beings to share in his glory and love. That seems to be why, as the Bible says, we are made in the image of God. (Genesis 1:26-28)

The way of the Trinity can be seen as similar to the nature of people. A man and a woman truly in love have no need for children. They are happy as a couple. Yet they often wish for children with whom they can share their love. When children come into such a family they are welcomed, cared for and loved. They share in all the things of the family. Is it possible that God wants us to share forever with Him in His family?

# Why People Don't and Why They Do Go to Church

There are many different reasons people cite for not attending any religious services. For some, there may be multiple reasons. For others, attendance was not part of their family culture and they never got into the practice of going to church. Today, more than in times past, there is a sizeable percentage of atheists who simply do not believe in God. Others believe God had something to do with creation but is not concerned with the day to day lives of people. Nevertheless, the name Jesus is known to almost all people today whether or not they believe in God. To say his name aloud in a mixed group is likely to bring a host of reactions that may be both positive and negative.

Despite the many different viewpoints that people hold, the power of the name Jesus is felt by practically everyone, regardless of their beliefs. The following is a list of some of the reasons people give for not going to religious services.

## Some Reasons Given for not Going

It's boring.

I don't get much out of going.

It interferes with things I'd rather do.

I used to go but don't like to take the time for it anymore.

They didn't seem very friendly at the church I went to.

I moved and never started going to a new church.

My family wasn't religious and neither am I.

I'm angry at God. He took my spouse, child, best friend far too early in life.

I'd rather spend the time doing other things that interest me more.

Why go? They give better sermons on TV.

I just don't believe much in religion or God.

I had a run in with some church people and won't be back.

When I was young, my parents made me go. Now, I don't have to.

I was personally hurt by a priest or minister.

I believe in God, but in my own way.

I live with a lifelong ailment. I'm not happy with God about that.

I'm just too busy to spend time in church.

I was really turned off from church by something the minister/priest said.

Weekends are the only time I have to relax.

I don't believe half the stuff they tell you in church.

It's been so long; I wouldn't know how to act in church.

The way my life's been going, I don't think I'd be welcome in a church.

Due to health reasons it's hard for me to attend.

They just want more people to put money in the collection basket.

I believe the Lord loves us whether we go or not.

I just don't believe in God.

My preferred church denomination is too far from me.

No particular reason, I just don't go to church.

I prefer to watch services on TV.

## Some Reasons for Attending

As with those who don't attend, there are a host of reasons given by those who do attend for them to keep returning on a regular basis to their chosen church.

I want to give thanks for all God's gifts in my life—family, friends, decent health, etc.

I've met friends at church that I enjoy seeing.

I want to come closer to God.

I want my children to have a good moral foundation.

God's word and the Gospel is important to me.

I'm proud but I gladly kneel to my creator and savior.

I'm glad I can help support the church and some worthy causes.

Going helps me to feel better when I find myself in personally difficult times.

I enjoy the music, the choir and the singing.

I'm glad to participate and to lend a hand sometimes with church functions.

Usually, I get something out of the sermons.

I'm not always in total agreement with the sermons but that's OK.

I go to please my spouse.

I believe God sent his son to die for us. That means a lot to me.

I believe God has a personal relationship with each of us including myself. We are all different.

God knows me and all my failings. He still loves me, immensely, and that makes me happy. That's why I want to worship Him.

# Epilogue

## A Way to go Forward

Christianity may be seen to be in crisis by those in Europe and the United States who have noted declining enrollments and participation in church services. However, Christianity is alive, well and even growing in many other parts of the world. Certainly, it is alive in the hearts and minds of the faithful. Many others look instead to science to continue to solve health problems and to make our world a comfortable place to live. Perhaps for some, faith in science has replaced faith in God. For those who have no religious background, particularly those who can be said to have a scientific way of looking at the world, the claims of religion may very well be difficult to accept. The resurrection of a man, Jesus Christ, from the dead is a case in point. That that man proclaimed himself to be the son of God belies any scientific explanation. It can only be accepted by faith alone. For some, that may be near impossible unless one has a rather shocking experience in life that can change one's world view. A long time ago it was said, "There are no atheists in foxholes." There may be much truth in that for when one's life is on the line, hope may only come with belief.

I find it hard to believe that a good God would condemn everyone who doesn't believe. People arrive at truth in different ways. Atheists and others can certainly lead good lives and may also be solicitous for the well-being of others. Those of us who are Christians would like to welcome them into our churches. We can invite, it is for them to accept or decline. Life is complicated today, probably more so than at any time in the past. Because we receive information from so many sources, it is easy to reach our own conclusions and feel we are making right choices. I don't think that God can be against us if we do right by others in following our own consciences as we live out our lives. Certainly, many people have little knowledge of the love of God the father and His son, Jesus.

No matter what our religious preference or lack of preference is, human beings in general want to do what they believe will make them happy. Americans live in a beautiful country with a great many positives. That being said, almost all people know that even in America there are some concerns and problems that affect a great many of us. Some that come to mind are mass murders, drug addiction leading to death and the high of cost health care. Adding to these major concerns are the strong feelings we have for the health of a loved one or for our own personal health. Furthermore, other cares, such as high costs, personal confrontations and disagreements can increase our stress levels and put us in a bad frame of mind. In general, most of us could use some relief from concerns and if health care people are right, exercise, spending time on a hobby, limiting hours spent on social media and increasing time with friends and family can all be helpful ways to reduce stress.

Prayer and meditation are also recognized to have a calming effect in our lives. Prayer takes a certain amount of faith while meditation requires none. Prayer and meditation are both easy to do and can be done when time is quite limited or for a half hour or even for an hour or more. Most Christians, Muslims and Jews know how to pray, though the practice of meditation may not be as familiar. However, anyone can benefit from the power of meditation, including atheists and agnostics, to help reduce stress and promote equanimity.

## Meditation

Let's first look at meditation and then go on to prayer. Taking some time for meditation is a recommendation frequently made by counselors and psychologists to help in dealing with stressful times and situations. It is a way to come to a more relaxed frame of mind. Below are simple instructions on how to do it from mindful.org, a company dedicated to sharing the gifts of mindfulness through content, training, courses, and directories.

"Meditation is simpler (and harder) than most people think. Read these steps, make sure you're somewhere where you can relax into this process, set a timer, and give it a shot:

**1) Take a seat**

Find place to sit that feels calm and quiet to you.

**2) Set a time limit**

If you're just beginning, it can help to choose a short time, such as five or 10 minutes.

**3) Notice your body**

You can sit in a chair with your feet on the floor, you

can sit loosely cross-legged, you can kneel—all are fine. Just make sure you are stable and in a position you can stay in for a while.

**4) Feel your breath**

Follow the sensation of your breath as it goes in and as it goes out.

**5) Notice when your mind has wandered**

Inevitably, your attention will leave the breath and wander to other places. When you get around to noticing that your mind has wandered—in a few seconds, a minute, five minutes—simply return your attention to the breath.

**6) Be kind to your wandering mind**

Don't judge yourself or obsess over the content of the thoughts you find yourself lost in. Just come back.

**7) Close with kindness**

When you're ready, gently lift your gaze (if your eyes are closed, open them). Take a moment and notice any sounds in the environment. Notice how your body feels right now. Notice your thoughts and emotions.

**That's it! That's the practice**. You focus your attention, your mind wanders, you bring it back, and you try to do it as kindly as possible (as many times as you need to)."

In addition, another one of the many good comprehensive sources on meditation is, https://psychcentral.com/health/meditation-for-beginners This site provides a wealth of information on the proven advantages of meditation, as well as on some of the various types of meditation.

## Prayer

In some ways prayer is easier than meditation. In grade school, nuns taught their students to make what they called "ejaculations," such as "Jesus, I love you," "Lord help me," "Jesus, Mary and Joseph," "Lord, look down with kindness on me," etc. One I especially like is "Jesus, meek and humble of heart, make my heart like Thine." These simple one line prayers can be said at any time of the day or night.

For those who are beginners in prayer the hardest part may be getting started. Obviously, one needs a quiet place, especially as God is not going to talk out loud to us. If one is not experienced, an easy way to get started is to find a place where you're not distracted and simply begin with "Lord help me." That is a way of opening the door. The next step is to listen to what He will say to you. Then, you can tell Him just what is on your mind. If you are fearful, ask Him to help with that. If you have a major concern or concerns let Him know what they are and ask for His help with them. Don't be afraid to ask, and when you have finished praying don't forget to be thankful that God would listen to you. Also, don't think that with one prayer your problems will be solved. Things take time and very often God works in ways that you might not expect.

Whatever you do, don't be afraid to come back again and again in prayer with God. Let Him know if you're frustrated at how things are going. Even let Him know if you feel your prayers haven't been answered. It's definitely OK to let God know what you think. Sometimes it will take patience. And, if your prayers have been answered, be sure to thank and praise God.

Besides informal prayers there are many formal and traditional prayers starting with the "Our Father," and including all kinds of prayers in prayer books and in the Bible. Reading one or more of the many psalms in the Bible can be especially meaningful. Some you may find don't apply to your particular situation while others you may discover will be right on for you. It's important to try to give your best attention, despite distractions, to any prayer for your prayer to be meaningful, and it's also important to be thankful that God listens and that you can actually have a personal relationship with Him. Be open to His suggestions. Don't expect that with prayer your life will suddenly be turned around but be patient for in time if you come to love Jesus, the Son of God, you will find happiness in life.

## Note

If one who has not been attending has the desire to go to a church, doing so may initially seem somewhat daunting. It may take a bit of courage. If a friend asks one to go with him or her that would likely make it much easier. Of course, a person who wants to go could just as well ask to join a friend who attends services.

Whatever we do or don't do it is good to remember that God loves each person individually far more than we ever could. He is actually more solicitous for our happiness and salvation than we are. However, He also is very much aware that sin may bring us passing pleasure but not happiness. All of us, the good and the not so good, are in the end headed toward death. God in His goodness and patience wants each of us to join with Him in the unending life of eternal happiness.

If you liked this book, or if not, consider taking a minute or two to leave a review on Amazon. Why? It lets others know what people think, and more reviews increase the visibility of the book. It's done through Amazon algorithms that help a book to come up when people are looking for works on similar topics.

To give a review, find the book on Amazon. Giving a review is easy to do, and is completely confidential unless you choose to include your name. To do so, find the book on Amazon and then scroll down looking on the left until you see customer reviews. Under that is "Review product." Right under review product is an elongated circular box with the word inside it "write a review." By clicking there 5 stars appear and if you think the book is good you click on the star to the far right. Then there's more you can add, and you can even write a review in your own words. A short line or two is fine. If reviewing my fiction, please don't give away the happy ending. When you're done, with the stars or complete review, be sure to click the yellow **submit** button below for it to register. And, thank you very much. (See next page)

**Important Note:** Unfortunately, Amazon won't accept reviews unless one has purchased $50 worth of Amazon merchandise within the last 12 months.

## About the Author

Tom is of Hungarian and Slovak heritage and he and both his parents were born and lived their lives in Indiana. After serving in the United States Army as an electronic technician in Turkey and Germany, Tom returned home and later met a lovely Irish girl who caught his fancy. Before long, he fell in love with her. Three months later the two were engaged and five months later they married, joining together to have four children, two daughters and two sons.

After working for many years for the State of Indiana as a job counselor and job finder for the unemployed, Tom considered himself fortunate when he was able to retire early. More than anything, he wanted to write both fiction and topics of practical and religious interest for himself and others. In nonfiction his easy-to-read writing style may have come from his father, a technical writer, who translated engineering concepts into common language used by equipment operators and repair personal. Tom's research on religious topics has been for historical accuracy and insight into the life of Christ and his mother, Mary.

Tom's fiction is mostly historical, usually with a strong heroine and brave hero who might just fall in love. His novels are full of adventure and to date they have been enjoyed by many adults and teens.

# Books

## Some of Tom's books and novels

To check them out further enter Tom Molnar
in books on Amazon.

**Time out for Happiness:** Proven ways and means to bring more happiness into our lives.

**Mist on the Moon:** A prince, a lady, a stable boy and the attacking Magyars. This is the most personable of Tom's novels featuring engaging characters and a younger sister whose bubbly nature is a joy—most of the time.

**Jesus, Kind, Loving, Dangerous:** Insight into Jesus' life and mission as it applies to us today.

**Swept Away:** A novel. Life, love and fighting during the American Civil War. How the war affected Jenny, the man she has her sights on, and Americans living in the midst of conflict.

**Mary the Girl Who Said Yes** A tribute to the life of the Blessed Virgin Mary. Praised by a bishop a priest and a nun.

**Wired for Love:** Removing barriers to getting and giving love.

**The Universe of God and Humanity:** Is it evolution, God's plan or something else controlling the amazing world in which we live?

**Dark Age Maiden:** A willful young woman, a knight, a count and the battle to save Europe from the advancing Saracen army. Set in a time of major historical import.

**Dark Age Woman:** Sequel to Dark Age Maiden

**A Quick Look at Heaven:** A look at what awaits us in heaven including some findings from near death experiences.

www.ingramcontent.com/pod-product-compliance
Lightning Source LLC
LaVergne TN
LVHW020639100826
845148LV00012B/2241

* 9 7 8 1 7 3 4 3 5 9 3 5 0 *